Rouault

Ro

uault

Translated from Romanian as published by
MERIDIANE PUBLISHING HOUSE
Bucharest, 1975
under the original title of
ROUAULT

Anthology of texts,
selection of illustrations and chronology by
IRINA FORTUNESCU

Translated into English by
RICHARD HILLARD

GEORGES ROUAULT
Notes and Correspondence

SOLILOQUIES

Like a peasant tied to his land, I am attached to my pictorial soil, like the man hanged by his hempen rope, like an ox under his yoke, labouring on, tooth and nail, never raising my eyes from my canvas save to assess the light, the shadow, the half-tints, the strange features of some pilgrims, recording every form, colour or fleeting harmony, until they are all so indelibly printed in my memory that they will stay for ever with me, even beyond the grave.

Some works of art are doomed from their very birth, to be the object of abuse. That my painting should stir scandal has never been my purpose. I have never aimed at scandal, never sought polemics, nor have I ever wished to shock or harm anyone. There are some, however, who take me for a monster loathing all mankind, a monster who deliberately wills the world to be vile and despicable! No, not for the world shall they be able to force me to set on canvas thoughts alien to my nature. They have never grasped the heartfelt thoughts I cherish for humanity, which, they claim, I revile and scoff at. They have never heard, whether in time of war or of peace, as I did, the death-rattle of slaughtered animals, the nightmarish gasp of dying lips unable to utter a sound. Heavily bound to this earth, like old god Pan, I have seen millions of human creatures perishing in these merciless wars. Therefore, here I am, voiceless, glued to the ground, like a bird hypnotized by a serpent.

The richer an artist's fancy and the wilder his chase after chimera, the more imperative it is to be realistic: to develop and control his gift for observation, to record and store, with utmost accuracy, all forms and harmonies perceived every day; to learn to grasp them better; to juggle with them like toys.

The artist first strives to acquire riches, which he then sheds if he be blessed with grace.

In the arts, *to know* signifies nothing. In order to create again Mathias Grünewald's terrifying *Christ Crucified*, who, with taut hands and twisted legs, crooks the cross out of shape; in other words, in order to forge the drama anew, one must possess a faith as pure and strong as his!

The deeper the inwardness of an artist's vision, the more firmly must he seek the support of Nature.
The work of art, more than man realizes, is an act of Will. And yet, no matter how endowed an artist may be with the most monstrous will-power, he will never attain that ultimate target he aimed at.

Ugliness is not always what so many champions of standard beauty suppose it to be, but rather the reproduction in a hundred thousand copies, of a work of successful mediocrity.

THOUGHTS AND RECOLLECTIONS

The language of forms and colours has to be learnt with utmost earnestness; it calls for an entire life of dedication and above all genuine talent. Our whole life is spent humbly and lovingly searching to unravel the secrets of Nature and Humanity. How can we make the idle young princes of art understand this truth? Scarcely born, they expect us to proclaim their transcendental genius, which, in no more than a couple of months, will be breathing its last.

Painting is for me merely a means, like any other, of forgetting life. If I have constantly been reluctant to defend my concepts, it is because our language is made up of shapes, colours and harmony, and not of words. With no vain pride, I must confess I've had my reward; so then, why talk, explain or justify myself or, worse still, pass sentence upon others? Let them, condemn me or grant me mercy, as they wish! Oh Heavens! What can I do?

Do not speak about me, but rather extol the virtues of art; do not brand me as the blazing torch of revolt and negation. My sins are but scanty. I deserve not all this attention. What I have done: a mere cry in the night, a stifled sob, a strangled laugh. In the whole world, every day, thousands of obscure, needy toilers, who are worthier than I, die at their tasks.

In order to paint with the art of Fra Angelico, it is not enough to pray unto God before we take up the brush, nor to trust that spiritual means alone can achieve a lasting work of art. There must be, first and foremost, a genuine, powerful and steadfast calling.

Art is an option, a choice and an inner hierarchy. It is easy to demolish, but hard to build up again; there is, however, a false order which some people contrive to pass off as an ancient heritage. The trick however is far too obvious.

I am, by nature, submissive and dutiful, yet any man is liable to rebel; it is no easy task to humbly obey our inner calling and pass our lives searching for genuine means of expression compatible with our temperament and our craftsmanship, if such skill exists. I am not the man to cry "Neither God, nor Master" in order to assume the place of God whom I have banished.

Is it not more honest to be Chardin, or even some lesser artist than a pale and melancholy shadow of the great Florentine?

The machine has invaded the earth and the sky, it penetrates the bottom of the oceans and scours the most arid of deserts, heedless of desecrating the peace of early dawn. Everything moves ever faster, people have barely the time to heave a breath before giving up their ghost. The survival of art in this age of machines, is not a miracle?

A man of science was able to assert: "There is no mystery left in the world." One may be a great scientist and yet a great fool at the same time. For, in the realm of the spirit — where the artist ventures to roam — everything is imponderable; for this is a world of other values, beyond the control of the inspector of weights and measures.

The look in Rembrandt's aged eyes, or the death-mask of Beethoven are for me as soul-stirring as a whole century of heroic action. In point of fact, a thing of beauty is, and has always been, a mystery. It is the privilege of few to seek out this mystery; it is therefore their sacred duty to persist in the search for this beauty up to the end of their lives. He who embarks upon this quest will not be spared pain and torture, but his will be the attainment of a pure and supreme joy.

Despite his genius, Pascal was mistaken in his dictums on painting: we are not called upon to vie in brilliance with nature.

Even if there be nothing new under the sun, everything can be recast and transfigured: we may sing in a new manner, in musical modes different from those of the past. Virtuosi with dead souls, the hand is but the docile ancillary of the spirit ever alive and ardent.

The old canons, the graceful proportions, the serene balance of the classic Greek statues did not suffice. Next to the consummate specimens of that antique statuary there is a false Hellenic art, conventional and worthless. In the name of beauty we are showered with hackneyed stereotypes, for artists no longer watch nature nor observe the life and urges of the human being. There is rhythm and harmony everywhere for him who seeks it.

6

The medieval craftsman cherished his stone, his wood and carved it with love and devotion. Anonymous builders of our great cathedrals, were vastly superior to many pseudo-personalities of our day, now when the ideal collaboration between architect, painter and sculptor has been abolished. The art of cathedral building is at once collective and individual. But the way of life, the modes of feeling, understanding and loving that were at the root of this art, cannot be artificially revived. New things are being achieved, but we cannot attempt to build anew what only the spontaneous collective effort of generations was able to raise, inspired by the faith they passionately treasured.

You don't enter a Tradition the way you get on a bus waiting for your number to be called. It requires deeper and subtler affinities.

A painter of joy!... Why not? I was ever happy to paint; so mad about painting that I would forget everything even in my direst moments of distress. Critics were unable to perceive this because my subjects were tragic. Is it only in the subject we paint that we may find joy?

We are not modern because we paint topical subjects. We are not traditional because we broach heroic themes. We are not pornographic because we paint a prostitute. It's not the helmet that makes the fireman.

Study

Miserere
(Variant of Plate No. 18)
"The Condemned is Gone"

Order emerges from within not from without. The supreme form of righteousness is self-denial. Oh you, the rich, in your delusion, you believe you are redeemed, when all you have given away was but the overflow of your material wealth!

It was at the time I lived in Versailles. One day I caught sight of a woman in the doorway of a brothel. She looked divinely beautiful, wrapped in the bright colours cast by the sun. I made straight for home and set to painting her, *just as she was*. In applying my brushstrokes, I rediscovered the woman I had admired, for herself and for the sundry reasons that had stirred my admiration. Bloy used to say: "A saint or a trollop." I refuse to judge and pass sentence.

I was born a worker in a workers' district. I used to go to the Fernando Circus, where I made sketches of clowns, acrobats and showmen. But I never lived in their midst. I just watched them; but never with indifference. There are people who always suspect the existence of some shifty scheme or hidden purpose, . . . a gimmick as they call it today.

That cannot endure, one day you must decide to be true to yourself. Life is no gimmick. I was a stained-glass painter, who had seen nothing of life. I went to school, I painted, I went in for competitions, I was blind to everything around. Then suddenly I was plunged into life, face to face with direct emotions; it was no longer the walls of my workshop but life itself that I began to see, ever more clearly. From now on I will close my eyes and search into my inner self. I devoured libraries with the craving hunger of a primitive. My friends Suarès and Léon Bloy had no influence upon me. Bloy was in point of fact insensitive to plastic art, what he found interesting in my work, was only the religious subjects; the pictorial aspect escaped his grasp. I have never worked with the *Fauves*. The only artist to exert any influence upon me was Rembrandt.

I was often reproached for not having continued painting in my initial manner. I felt the need to create for myself. We must muster our ambition not for our sake or for the work already accomplished, but for that which has still to be achieved. In all I have done, I have been guided only by my nature. Have I been true to myself?

CORRESPONDENCE
To Edouard Schuré
(about 1905)

At the fall of dusk, after a lovely day, when the first star, shining in the heavenly vault sent a tremor through my heart, an entire world of poetry was born to me. That circus wagon of wondering gipsies halted on the roadside, the old jade browsing the sparse grass, the aging clown seated beside his van patching his glittering motley-coloured costume, *the contrast* between these scintillating garments of entertainment and this life, of *infinite sadness*, loomed before my eyes . . . And then I blew up the picture, and I suddenly recognized who the "clown" really was. It was I, you, practically *all of us* . . . This richly spangled costume is a gift dealt out by life; we are more or less all of us, *somewhat clowns*, wearing "a spangled costume". But if we are suddenly caught unawares the way I caught the old clown, why then, oh God! Who'd dare deny that his heart would be rent with infinite compassion? I have the mania, or the failing (if indeed it be a failing; in any case it is a source of ceaseless agony) of *stripping everyone of their glamorous or pompous spangled costumes*, be he King or Emperor: with my own eyes must I peer into the soul of the man before me and the more exalted his position, the more humbly worshipped he be, the greater my misgivings for his soul . . . I have let myself be carried away by my intimate thoughts. I know this road is fraught with danger, with pits and snares everywhere and once embarked upon this path it is more perilous to try and turn back than to continue one's trek . . . To draw the essence of your art from the sight of an old crock (man or horse), supposes either "boundless vanity" or "deepest humility", according to the clay you are made of.

To André Suarès
Paris, August 22, 1911

Life is a thrilling, soul-stirring powerful spectacle provided you succeed in discovering that creative substance that feeds the spirit and heart... I have set out upon this quest... a road whence I cannot return... I had to rely only upon myself, to draw all the energy from within and at times I wonder whether all these efforts, this dogged perseverance and all the sacrifices around me were really worth it?

Saturday evening 1927

Just as in my childhood I watched the shows in the fair, or at the age of fourteen, I stood spellbound before the old stained glass windows, oblivious of everything around and of my very self, I discovered that basic truth: a tree projected against the sky is as rich in interest, character and expression as the human countenance. But this truth must be proclaimed; and this is where the difficulty begins.

For the champions of objective art, the task is easy: they set off like an ox in harness, and carry on without a moment's hesitation.

I've seen quite a number of such "swatters", at work in the studio. Standing before the sitter, they would start from the tip of the hair on his crown and, before a week was over, the model was ready reproduced up to the last rosy tint of his right toe-nail.

When, at dusk, entranced, I saw the grey walls turn into silver in the waning light and the colour of flesh gain radiance with ever richer mellow hues, it was then that I felt how poor my powers were.

The quest for the magical effects of colour schemes is a joy both to the eye and to the mind, and yet it is also the leaden ball tied to the prisoner's feet, condemned to drag it along without respite.

Some kindhearted friends kept counselling me: *Nature? — You'll soon tire of it*. On the contrary, the impenitent visionary or the legendary poet, were he to live for thousands of ages, will never cease exploring nature in ever novel ways and nature will for ever be the springboard for new ideas and ventures.

To Georges Chabot
Paris, March 20, 1927

(...) Yes indeed, you have recognized the masters who guided my first steps. What's more what you have *recognized* is what I had never dared hope anyone would discern, so imperfect is my *achievement* compared with my *vision* (oft am I covered with shame for my inability to render it). So then, there are, after all, here and there some original and expressive features and an inner vision which may appeal not only to snobs or to those who cultivate the fashions of the day.

At times I feel as though I am sailing on Medusa's raft, on a chilly grey-skied day, shivering with cold, my teeth chattering. Shipwrecked alone, I thought that in pain and sorrow I would find peace and relief. This was not to be: there is no end to the agony of the dreamer who seeks to seize reality, refusing to be deluded by his wandering fancy.

However great they were and however humble our admiration for them, the old masters have not said everything. For him who watches and is not the slave of theories and preconceived doctrines, a visage, a look, a twinkle in the eye of an unknown passer-by can be a subject to work upon. The same is true for some landscape. Do you feel in you the vain pride, that you are creating? Not in the least. It is they who, resentfully taking umbrage at your searchings, force you to reassess your work, work which you had considered to be insignificant. And then, searching more closely, new tonalities more precious and more precise are revealed to you. Those who flatter you, do you no good, it is your enemies who by their excessive criticism render you a far more fruitful service.

The artist worthy of this name cherishes every grain of life. In an age both so distressing and so sublime as ours, when life demands of every man so much individual heroism and oft as much humility, can we blame an artist sensitive to the "profound poetry of life" to withdraw into his shell, seeking shelter, like a soldier in the trenches, from the cross-fire of so many contradictory theories, compromises, and impostures. And what's more, this can be easily done in the very midst of his environment, without retiring into a desert.

People talk about "Expressionism". Was I an Expressionist thirty years ago? People keep saying so but I was totally unaware of it, nor did I care what I was labelled. I was like a blind ox ploughing his furrow. I hope to finish the cycle *Miserere et Guerre*, you mentioned, in two or three years; we could exhibit a hundred works or so, but I have still a tremendous lot to do before it is completed.

No doubt, in my youth I was under Rembrandt's spell, then, at the age of thirty, I was suddenly seized with a sort of madness, or maybe favoured with a state of grace, according to one's viewpoint. Anyhow, "the image of the world changed entirely for me", if I might make so presumptuous a statement. I perceived everything I had seen before, in a different light and harmony. Is it the eye that deceives us at times?

And in this solitary world of mine I beheld a procession of clowns, tottering along weary and haggard, of Christs mocked and abused by the mob, Orpheus stripped to rags by Bacchantes. As I transferred these images to canvas, I poured into them, without any deliberate design, my own inner joy or more often my even deeper anguish. On reviewing these canvases today, canvases that are no longer mine, I begin to realize how bitterly I must have disappointed my contemporaries, in particular those who had fostered the hope that one day I would be "a worthy winner of a Prix de Rome."

This letter of mine is entirely superfluous: as you have already made up your opinion about my painting, it adds nothing in my favour; on the contrary it may only lower still more your estimation, since I am no gifted writer. No doubt you must have noticed that. And yet my drawers are filled with thousands of poems, of little significance though. If they do however possess any merit it is only inasmuch as they respond to an inner voice, a voice untainted by the complacent established standards of beauty cultivated by the artists of today, painters with great skill and hearts of stone.

April 1951

... No, I am not a *good* and righteous man, far from it. No. I cannot bear those sort of people who parade their goodness, hypocrites who brag about their righteousness.

No, I am not an inveterate and stupid *optimist* who turns a deaf ear and a blind eye to the realities of life.

No, I am not an *idealist*, easy to understand and follow, a mealy-mouthed idealist who flaunts his idealism like a banner in season or out of season, without rhyme or reason.

I have the proud feeling of living on a plane where *idealism and realism are intimately linked together*, so secretly as to rouse the indignation of the common objectivist and the idealist of the same ilk. Wonder not therefore, if I seem to shun the company of people, for I don't — it is not my style of life; what I do avoid and fear all the more is the contact with the *snobbish élite*.

ON ROUAULT

For this painter for whom art was "an ardent confession" and who, effectively, identified himself with his art, it is not surprising that his writings — which fortunately bore no trace of the standard professional man of letters — should incorporate his entire individuality, as a man, as a Christian and as an artist.

His style, as a writer, is genuinely his own. His language is replete with popular phrases (he is particularly fond of proverbs), archaisms and rare words, which perfectly befit the pen of a friend of Huysmans and of Bloy. The frequent omission of the article lend the phrases vivacity while the numerous methaphors add colour to the text. Prompted by the same need for picturesqueness, epithets abound. Generally coupled, they remind us of his paintings where likewise Rouault prefers to assemble two figures rather than three. And just as in his paintings, where the blue tonalities prevail, adopting yellow lines only when he was 80 and never employing red pigments except with utmost parsimony; so too in his poems, as well as in his prose, where assonances are abundantly present, he favours the subdued not the glaring sounds. The plaintive *I's*, the whispered *U's*, the mute *E's* are more to his liking than the *A's* and *O's*, which he never resorts to except to bring out, by contrast, the soft velvety tones. The result is a music not infrequently remindful of Verlaine's and which raises some of his poems almost to the height of masterpieces.

If, as a writer, he speaks of no one but himself, even when he believes he is commenting upon Ingres, Gustave Moreau, Degas and Cézanne, it is because as a man he is a paragon of selfcentredness. Ever since his childhood up to his old age, he was the prisoner of the École des Beaux-Arts where they strove in vain to instill into him the cult of Greek Art, Italian Art, Michelangelo and of "Dominique" — meaning Ingres. As to his horror of critics this can be readily explained by the attacks that these directed against his art, for ever so long a period. Under the appearance of a tough character, he was really an emotional and tender being, all the more vulnerable as he struggled to conceal his wounds.

No wonder therefore, that just like Degas and Cézanne, he too was a solitary artist — a maverick — determined to remain alone — the only means of preserving his freedom of spirit. Refusing to join any school, furious when art historians included him in some movement. He was a champion of independence, to such a degree that he refused all incorporation, even in the ranks of the rebels. To those who proclaimed: "Neither God, nor Master" he would reply that they too were slaves, the slaves of their revolt, whereas he, proclaiming his obedience, safeguarded more thoroughly the rights of man and his individuality. There is a close relationship between his writings and his art, manifest when we compare some of his texts with his canvases or etchings. The kinship is striking between his poems and his *Judges*, his *Maternities*, his *Barge* in the Grenoble Museum, *The Ticket-sellers of the Street Circus*, his *Miserere* and his *Lady of High Society* . . . "It is the same Rouault torn between agony and bliss."

BERNARD DORIVAL, 1971

From the canvases sent by Mr. Rouault, only one was accepted, *The Dead Christ Mourned by the Holy Women*. The painting, which caused so great a stir when it appeared last year at the School of Fine Arts, among the compositions competing for the Prix de Rome. There is in them a clear evidence of the painter's passionate devotion to the great masters. Where his genius, however, breaks forth is in the strict orderliness of the composition and in the choice of that all-pervading sumptuous green tonality that intensifies the horror of the drama. Casting an all round glance over the ten paintings, one is struck by the remarkable contrasts they display: it is also an abundant evidence of the outstanding superiority of Moreau's school over the training imparted in other workshops.

ROGER MARX
La Revue Encyclopédique, 1896

Were I not so utterly convinced of the integrity and noble character of Mr. Rouault, the curator of the Moreau Museum, and were I not so fully conscious of the genuine value of his powerful Hogarth-like syntheses, — a terrifying pageantry whence anguishing eyes stare forth — I would certainly not stand up to defend him against the sneering mob that cluster before his three or four "black canvases". I know that his spirit is pure and his heart heavy: when he paints a prostitute he does not crudely relish, like Lautrec, the vicious thrill emerging from this creature, but suffers an agony and sheds tears. Oh, you painter of darkness, what a distressing vision! Are those, by any chance, negresses in a tunnel? Or is it perhaps an illustration for the newspaper "The Invisible"? One can distinguish nothing; nothing save a paste made up of caviar, blacking and pitch . . . What sort of light is there in Mr. Rouault's studio? What over-smoked glasses conceal nature and life to this mysoginous dreamer who plunges into the depths of Erebus?

LOUIS VAUXCELLES
Gil Blas, October 14, 1904

Mr. Rouault exhibits sinister canvases. These horrifying caricatures of Gustave Moreau's works rouse compassion. One can't help wondering what inhuman urge prompts the artist to conceive such paintings.

GUILLAUME APOLLINAIRE
L'Intransigeant, 1910

Rouault is a powerful painter, whom I have repeatedly judged unfairly.

GIULLAUME APOLLINAIRE
Le Petit Bleu, February 9, 1912

He now regards his contemporaries with a troubling and hostile eye. He hates them. One is apt to infer that discouraged by finding that the seraphic figures he had first sought, proved not to be true to life, he is now taking his revenge delineating the human species with censorious scorn.

His vigor is undeniable in the powerful and sombre harmonies looming in purple-tinted darkness. His vigor is undeniable in his distortions where the human bodies appear as wrecks frantically tossed about by a Juvenal-like painter. The application of his grim paintings to ceramics has produced totally novel effects. It is not one of his least merits to have thus been an innovator. Is this violent satirical art Mr. Rouault's last word? His is a fertile spirit; the old man with his emotional temper, the poet of his early days, might awaken again, and we would indeed be faced with a strange message should Mr. Rouault return to the Garden of Eden after having scoured the depths of Hades.

GUSTAVE KAHN
Mercure de France, 1912

They were not fully remarked, last year, at the exhibition held at the Druet Gallery: Rouault's "Albums" where horrible, anguishing, drawings, laden with compassion and irony, alternate with bitter, lashing comments, strange poems that recall those recited in the Umbrian villages by the followers of St. Francis of Assisi, those *Giullari di Dio*, the minstrels of God, whose songs rose heavenward with a new soul-rending lyricism . . .

Since Daumier few painters have attained that height of sublime comedy which here is reached by sublime tragedy.

GUILLAUME APOLLINAIRE
L'Instransigeant, July 5, 1914

With his pale face, light coloured deep-searching eyes, ever intensely focused upon his object, sensuous lips, arched brow and domed skull, in his youth richly

12

covered with curly fair hair ... he bears the air of a lunatic clown — odd mixture of compassion and bitterness, malice and candour, all mirrored in the countenance of this painter, the declared enemy of all coteries, conventions and contemporary dogmas ...

It is generally said that he is a man of a nasty temper, unsociable above all. Indeed, he is none too easy to get on with, in particular if we ignore that the sophisticated procedure of affected civility is not the most felicitous approach. Nor if, with ill-required zeal, we venture to ask his opinion on new trends in painting or poetry, or where he plans to spend his holidays, what canvas lies on his easel, what he thinks of Franz Jourdain, what he paints with or oh! if above all we end up with: "I should love to see your latest works, when could I drop in at your studio?" Any of these overtures would be unpardonable.

He possesses furthermore also a strange bent for moral prozelytism, a genuine inability to accept the mediocrity of his fellow-creatures. Strangely, an unquenchable sympathy for everything human prompts this solitary artist to seek the company of his fellow-men, but then to express his indignation when he discovers their inevitable failings. Under this appearance of brusqueness, or even brutality, lies a heart that is never indifferent or disdainful to man's woes. This is the source of those grim forbidding images, more hideous than common caricature, whereby, in a certain (already remote) period he sought to unburden his outraged soul.

The most violent outbursts against the bourgeoisie (alas! how little he has in common with René Johannet's generation!) and our social order reflect at the same time the deep disappointment of a spirit, which, cherishing a moral discipline, nurtures the hope to encounter it in the street, the subway or the law-courts ...

Rouault possesses an almost Jansenistic *purity* that can however turn into cruelty, which constitutes both his force and his freedom; he carries within him a hidden spring of life, a profound religious sentiment, the faith of an unyielding ascetic that led him to Huysmans and Bloy, and which make him see in every outcast or woebegone creature the divine lamb, upon whom he bestow his tenderest compassion. If we add to these attributes his uncannily perceptive eye and ruthless critical spirit we cannot fail to understand the true source of his raging reactions.

But above all he is an artist and, without the shadow of a doubt, the most authentic, the most exclusive among the contemporary painters. We mean not only by his craftsmanship, and his perplexing artistry, but in the spirit of his painting, permeated by a vivid intellectual and sensitive reality. A philosopher could study in him the virtue of art in its pure state, with all its demanding and exclusive features.

If he offends many by his intransigence, if he defends his mettlesome and haughty independence, against a whole series of servitudes, he does it in order to preserve unadulterated the integrity of these virtues. He oft quotes Poussin's statement: "Ours is a silent art", and though thousands of ideas are seething in his mind, though he often finds the most suggestive words in appraising the genius of the old masters ... never does he attempt to explain his own art, leaving his work to defend itself, respecting the sanctity of art by never sullying it with words. Toiling on doggedly upon his own path, he cannot be classed as pertaining to any school.

His paintings, so human and expressive, reveal an exclusively plastic eloquence, destitute of any literary by-product. His love for precious materials might have carried him away into the meanders of endless searching, his humanistic bent and his gift of satire might have led him to cultivate the anedoctal. Suppressing neither, he succeeded in mastering both, lending ever greater forcefulness and purity to his art.

JACQUES MARITAIN, 1925

The man who — consciously or not — is guided by the thought of death is not necessarily a creature in despair. Death invests life with a peculiar sense — that is all; its purpose is not lamentation, rather the revelation of the absurd. I am certain that Mr. Rouault is most deeply haunted by this threatening thought. There is at present no work of art more destitute of love than the lay work of this Christian painter; as though love could not be expressed otherwise than by the image of Christ.

It is Christ — and not God — who redeems the believer, delivering him from the absurd.

Others, more qualified, will speak about Rouault's Christian paintings more competently than I can ... What I wish to underline, however, is that his entire range of canvases, his entire world, appears alien to us and unintelligible only if we refuse to approach his world in some of the most vital issues of human existence. No doubt, any great painter is subject to multiple interpretations, just because of his greatness. I am constantly surprised whenever Rouault is placed next to Daumier. I for one consider them at opposite poles: for Daumier there is but one world, the world of man: ranging from Don Quixote down to Sancho Panza, from the man who makes up for these failings by his own common sense (with judges and bourgeois, in his stride), never trespassing beyond the confines of the particular, the individual or the professional. Daumier's art is a quest for possession. He is the master of the model, which he wishes to portray and by so doing to rule.

In spite of the erroneously termed "picturesqueness" of his subjects, Rouault's models do not exist: they are but a potentiality, they will be that which his brushwork— at times crude and thickly laid, other times kneaded as in the stained glass windows of the Chartres — will make of them. Every character is reduced to what becomes of him after a tragic meditation upon his existence. Behind this trinity of parodies: the trollop, the clown, the judge, behind all these grim countenances, looms the shadowy cemetery of Basel, that sets its seal upon this Dance of Death.

There can be no more eloquent demonstration of how little Rouault's work is subjected to the outer world, than by placing side by side the painter's canvases and the people he pictures. In the Law Courts we can find Daumier's judges, in Spain we can meet Goya's mountebanks, in the suburbs we can discover Vlaminck's townscapes; but Rouault's judges, prostitutes or clowns cannot be found anywhere except in Rouault's canvases, just like Grünewald's characters that never really existed. They are not human beings, they are symbols by means of which man's spirit is freed from its obsessions; they are an act of exorcism. They are not symbols of plastic art: Rouault is not a man who strives *to see*, but a man who strives *to be*.

It is through this that Rouault is different from practically all the painters of his day. He does not expect to find a balance in his colours, but a *significance*; his art is not expressed in terms of beauty but in terms of existence. Just as Michelangelo challenged the dust of death by painting the superhuman figure of sibyls, so does Rouault proclaim his challenge, calling his fellow-beings to contemplate the sinful baseness of man and the merciful grace of Christ. It is a private act, a work of reason, in no way the concern of the beholder; the work of a dumb human being, maybe a masochist, who is driven to God by human suffering and who is well aware that he can never come to terms with this world.

Finally there's the call of art: because you cherish the value of shapes and are aided by a professional training — you grope in the darkness for other human beings, seeking a bond with the world of differences, to mark the breach between you and the world you accuse, your confrontation with the absolute ...

Uccello, an artist more solitary than Rouault, for totally different reasons, expects some privileged viewer to confirm his genius. The very fact that people interested in patches of colour, should come and view an exhibition of Rouault's paintings is surprising in itself. And yet fifty canvases on show could serve as an initiation into this world of tragedy where the artist moves with the pathetic staggering step of a paralytic. To admire an isolated canvas of Rouault's however, as one admires a Renoir for instance, only goes to prove to what abberation, indiscrimate admiration may lead one. Rouault is incorporated in his work, just as Rimbaud is in his *Illuminations*. Both declare to God that they refuse the world that He has created: Rimbaud is great enough to stand alone in silence where the last heroes spit at one another, whilst the response from Rouault's God is: "There is a Satan *too*."

ANDRÉ MALRAUX, 1929

In the dispersal of the Quinn collection three years ago Rouault's work brought some of the most miserable figures of the sale. All of the choice pieces went back to Europe. Despite which, today, even in Paris, a first-rate Rouault is not to be had.

This latter scarcity, however, is easily explained: M. Vollard, the market godfather of Cézanne and Renoir, has taken to Rouault. Or, rather, to be more literal and, at the same time, more exact, he has taken Rouault to himself; and taken him so thoroughly that for the last half-dozen years his output has been wrapped in a mysterious seclusion. Not that this state of things is in any way antipathetic to the master himself. He, personally, is reputed to have a "*sale caractère*", which in all probability means nothing more than he is unsociable. A notorious recluse reticent, timid, yet explosive . . .

Still on the rare occasions when one of his more recent works is offered to public scrutiny — as happened in 1929 when M. Vollard lent his epochal *Crucifixion* to the charity exhibition at La Renaissance in Paris — only a dazzled murmur of appreciation is audible. It is no longer "*les ébauches de mon ami Rouault*", as the poet Bloy described his works two decades back. Now it is the "drawing of a man who puts his finger in a pot of paint and smears it round the canvas." Rouault apprenticed as a boy to a stained glass worker, later, Rouault, the ceramist, medieval in spirit and sympathies, stands as today one of the first masters of modernism." Some months ago his *Crucifixion* shared a wall in the Rue Royale with Cézanne's monumental *Bathers* and halved the glory. Now his decor makes an important part of what Diaghileff terms the "Parsifal of Russian Ballet" — Prokofiev's "Prodigal Son" — recently produced in London.

But Rouault's still remains no easy beauty. And the reason for those years of tepid acceptance is not difficult to understand. His will never be a popular art. He is too uncompromising in style, even as he is uncompromising in temperament. A Celt and mystic, he seeks his beauty in a spiritual category rather than in a natural one. That is to say, while his ideal of beauty remains a plastic form, he requires that it expreses a spiritual vitality exciting to the senses rather than an organic vitality pleasing or reposeful to them. Here he is directly in the Gothic tradition.

Perhaps this is why he seems to stand so alone in a contemporary school, the characteristic of which is more often than not a happy synthesis of Northern and Southern ideals. At any rate, it is by considering him in this light that we come to the most sympathetic understanding of his work. Power of expression rather than beauty of expression is his aim. And to compass this end, like the Gothic masters themselves, he adopts as his prime plastic medium the linear.

Daumier was probably his most immediate kinsman in recent years. His simplifications are notably related to the former's work. However, while Daumier himself has a genius for the plastic line, Rouault carries his achievements even further, and through his individuality in this province stands as one of the most original of present-day painters.

JAMES SWEENEY
New York Times, April 6, 1930

Matisse is obsessed by the achievement of an aesthetic balance. Unlike the former, Rouault is the type of literary, sentimental Fauve, an Expressionist who derives his stylizations principally from caricature. Caricature that emerges from his catholic indignation. He is a stern and fiery preacher whose words however may sound monotonous but who is so overwrought that he gets choked in the excitement of his impassioned outcry.

In Rouault's paintings, frequently merely outlined, the figures barely stand out from the dark background, where they float and merge in the pasty or pale colours characteristic of the stained glass painter or ceramist. Apocalyptic mash. Rouault's works barely exceed the stage of a preliminary sketch; his canvases give the impression of blown-up prints. He utilizes the paint for anecdotal characterisations, and yet he asserts: "A black toque and a red robe make up such lovely spots of colour; it needs nothing more: His Honourable Justice might quietly go to bed."

He furthermore paints narrow streets lined with bawdy houses, steeped in the melancholy atmosphere of the morning hours, deserted by their clients; Versailles, the park with its terraces, is converted in his canvases into a phantomatic scene while the artesian fountain bubbles idly surrounded by grotesque spectres. Everything is but wanton waste.

It is with the eyes of a fervent catholic that he paints the prostitutes, denouncing the worthlessness of lewd flesh. It is the deliberate anathema of the mortal sin rather romantically thundered out. Rouault, too, painted an Olympia, but in a mortalizing tone, as a prostitute; in the background, in a wash-tub two other women are washing themselves: polluted beauty . . .

His clowns are tragic portraits of ill-treated, wretched ludicrous creatures. His judges are set next to the old strumpet dressed up as a bride — Justice in a Dance of Death. Degas rendered these subjects with cool detachment. Lautrec was more strongly engaged in his themes. Rouault is possessed by a monk-like wrath against this world: it is not worth yielding to its lures. This moralist has seldom risen beyond a hybrid caricature in expressing his creed. His work is a pathetic sermon.

KARL EINSTEIN, 1931

Rouault stands . . . in the essential line of French painters, drawing with a sense of form that reaches back to the Leonardesque tradition in which he began, using colour with a sense of the richness of that magical element proper to the land of Chardin, and also, however dark some of his pictures may be, using color that could only appear in the world after the Impressionists had made their great analysis of its properties. One needs to see the earlier Rouault pictures to realize how the heavy reds and blues he employs today are based on a knowledge of colour relationships that derives from Cézanne's synthetizing of the brilliant hues which, in his youth, he worked out with Pissarro and Monet.

Drawing for "Ubu"

Rouault is a man of his time on the technical side of his art: he belongs with his splendid group. It is when we consider him from the other standpoint, for the quality of expression in his work, that we can see what he meant when once he said: "I do not feel as if I belong to this modern life on the streets where we are walking at this moment, my real life is back in the age of the cathedrals. Lest these words appear boastful or affected, I would say that they were spoken in private, to a friend, who took them in the matter-of-fact way that the painter uttered them.

. . . .

A few years ago Paris smiled a very broad smile over Rouault presenting himself as a candidate for election to the Institute. Why this wild man, this *Fauve*, thinking of a seat among the forty Immortals? "Why not?" replied Rouault, when interviewed by a journalist, "I am a pupil of Gustave Moreau, who was a member of the Institute." It is reported that he did not receive one vote for the honour which went to Maurice Denis. Even that election testifies to some progress over the miserable record of France's official choices in the past; it also tells, however, that the day when originality and power will be the tests for preference has not yet come.

When we compare Rouault with the artists who are trying to restore religious painting to the place it held in former periods we see that it is just his combination of originality and power that distinguishes him from this group, even as it is his visionary quality that makes him stand out from the "pure painters" among whom he is more exactly to be classed. Religious painting has fallen to so low a state, that the weak men who are almost its sole practitioners, Severini, however, being a distinguished exception, have less in common with Rouault than those who have grown up in a school based on nineteenth century realism. The validity of its art is still apparent in the work of the artist we are considering. If he has painted Christ-figures of an impressiveness scarecely second to that of the mediaeval men, he has also told of Law the Courts with a vehemence which inevitably recalls that of Daumier, and which is a sufficient commentary on the hollowness of Forain.

His scenes of city streets, of the women who walk them, of the hard light on square buildings and the harder light on rouged faces, his wild but inescapable renderings of gaunt trees and livid skies are all testimonies to his being born in the period of naturalistic observation sixty years ago. The firm modelling is that of a school that remembers Courbet; the colour recalls that of the old glass painters and enamellers, but it is also a thing to he understood as a direct outgrowth of the scientific outlook which was almost universal during his boyhood, and not as an attempt to rejoin the things of the museum, the futile effort of men too weak to stand the impact of the great art of modern times. The readiness to use such exaggeration of drawing and character as we usually think to be only within the province of the caricaturist is typical of the time which finds one of its culminations in Brancusi. Be it said in passing that when the Autumn Salon was finding Rouault too strong a meat for the increasingly delicate stomach that has made it the weak show it is today, another sculptor of the type so loosely called modern, Duchamp-Villon, made a protest to the committee of the society and forced a fairer placing of Rouault's work, which the more poor-spirited members wanted to keep out.

It is clear that an art based so largely on the expression of ideas, taking the word in a literary sense, would lend itself perfectly to illustration. It is clear I have just said, and yet it remained for Ambroise Vollard to provide a fitting opportunity for Rouault to give this measure of his genius, and I believe that the word is not too strong.

WALTER PACH, January 1933

Condemned to total incomprehension by the sombre horror of his work, this artist would be still vegetating in his solitary studio, were it not for the irresistible power of the art dealers, the sole guides of artistic taste in France (and soon all the world over), who imposed Rouault's abstruse art upon the public. It is most likely that, before 1910, the young German art students, passing through Paris, beholding the works of Othon Friesz and in particular of Rouault — more alluring to them for its morbidity — should have experienced a revelation that subsequently generated their famous Expressionism. This art is now returning to us — maybe because of my imprudence in having labelled some works exhibited at I don't remember what Salon, as "French Expressionism"; works which appeared to me as particularly eloquent owing to certain systematic distortious more consistent with the Franco-Flemish Gothic canons than with the Greek-Latin tenets.

ANDRÉ LHOTE, 1933

After Jarry, it was the turn of M. Ambroise Vollard to rediscover Master Ubu... M. Ambroise Vollard has had the courage of reintroducing this personage with its full dictatorial bearing in a sort of burlesque revue, entitled *The Reincarnations of Master Ubu*. Without a moment's hesitation, M. Vollard picked out the artist best fitted to illustrate his work. In point of fact Rouault is here in his most natural surroundings. Is he not the habitual historiographer, the faithful portrayer of Ubu? Are his characters not a part of that mock-heroic world represented by Ubu? Rouault is the only artist who, investing caricature and the grotesque with greater significance, has dedicated himself to the world of drama. The universe created by him pictures the circus and the Inferno at the same time.

His concepts have been perfectly served by the rough technique of wood-engraving. The contrast between the opaque masses and the white surfaces bring out the crudeness of the characters. The hero bears a fairly vile mask, the coarse features betoken conceit and dullness of mind. His bearing is generally stiff, nailed down by his own reasoning, enclosed like a stained glass figure in the thickly traced contour of his silhouette. He seems to be aware of the charcoal shell in which he is confined. Master Ubu is constantly in the foreground, filling the entire space of his existence, concealing all trace of the backcloth. He reigns almighty, there is room for no other ruling spirit other than his. The minor characters belong to a species of non-vertebrates. Their appearance reflects shapes where the human form is largely distorted by the artist's symbolic intentions. They swarm about waving their arms in frenzy. Every part of their body is a larva, and the mass of larvae penetrates our imagination with tentacular force. The tense feeling of the prehensile power of these bodies is violently contrasted with the rigidity of the masks — no tentacle, however grasping, could avert the staring eyes riveted upon their target. At times these human silhouettes are confused with some strange trees or shrubs suggesting a decor of the fringes of a charred, burnt-out forest. There can be no salvation for those who are to descend into this inferno. The expert torturers and the contaminated idiots are already in training for the future torments of the doomed. In the artist's vision they are steeped in a tenebrous landscape, crossed by dark-coloured modulations. It is a sort of midnight storm that sweeps across the canvas and builds up, with vibrating hatches, the back-cloth for the performance of this sinister puppet: Ubu. Rouault's aquatints mark with even greater relief the incidents of the show; they have been executed in a manner to harmonize with the woodcuts and prints. At the end of the book, Rouault offers woodcuts of the subjects rendered in aquatint in the inset plates.

We have rarely witnessed a more admirable quality of woodcuts, with their unprecedented velvety smoothness. Every shade sought by the artist is set forth,

Plate for
"Les Réincarnations du Père Ubu"
by Ambroise Vollard

while the shades of the background have their own harmonic vibrations. In order to achieve these results, the common presses proved insufficient, even when operated by two men. The pressure was not strong enough, and the ink laid in too great quantity, clotted. For this reason Aimé Jourde, the press-man, ordered a special press for these sets, operated both electrically and manually with a minimum amount of ink; its highly delicate dosage enabled the rendering of a wide gamut of shades.

MARCEL ZAHAR, 1933

Rouault's astonishing talents which set him apart from, if not above, all other living European artists, have long been recognised in England, but the exhibition arranged by the Mayor Gallery makes it for the first time possible to trace his development and test his achievements in tangible example. The exhibition is uneven in quality, but it contains enough of his important works to make a visit there, not merely desirable, but essential.

During the last hundred years any artist born with a keen moral sense has found himself in an intolerable position. If Rouault had been born in the Middle Ages he would have found a system of thought, moral and philosophical, ready formed for him and armed with the ideals of the Catholic Church, he would probably have been one of the great anonymous masters of mediaeval Christian art... In the eighteenth century he would have found the world marching forward by means of Doubt, and he would have thrown in his lot with that great group of Frenchmen who, at any rate, saw clearly enough what to demolish in the old system even if they were uncertain about what should replace it. By the middle of the nineteenth century the situation had changed. Courbet attempted to be progressive and at the same time to face serious moral and social problems, but, after him, artists in general gave up the struggle, and with Impressionism begins that long stage in the history of the arts when painters devoted themselves to their own particular problems and progress was a matter of pigment, not of ideas.

There were, of course, still artists who continued to feel keenly about the vital problems of existence, but they were forced into isolation and into a purely negative attitude. Daumier, one of the most sympathetic figures of the century, attacked savagely and brilliantly the abuses around him. Forain, his spiritual heir, narrowed his range, but by concentrating on certain particular themes, such as the corruption of the French legal system, was enabled to keep up his intensity. The attitude of Lautrec is slightly different. There can be no doubt that he disapproved of the scenes of vice and squalor which he saw, and yet at the same time he revelled in them. His satire is therefore not less intense than, say, Forain's, but it is less detached.

In the present century the tradition of these satirical painters is carried on by Rouault and Grosz...

In the years from 1905 up to the War, Rouault, was the greatest satirical artist living. Since the War, others, such as Grosz, have arisen to rival him, but, sadly enough, his own powers seem to have waned. His passion seems colder and his means of expression cruder. In looking at his later works it is possible to ask whether he is not now doing from habit what he once did by conviction.

ANTHONY BLUNT
The Spectator, October 18, 1935

Rouault's works reflect a constant dedication; they represent a symbol, a necessity and above all a destiny. Malraux was the only critic who — most likely owing to their spiritual affinities — distinguished the essential quality of Rouault's art, fundamentally different from the analytical masterpieces of Daumier, with whom he was frequently compared.

Raising the themes to loftier planes, broadening the range of his subjects, discarding accessories and details, he has gradually recast his models into types of eternal value. From his early beast-like figures he has passed to hieratic motifs, without however losing the emotional suggestion of predestination. His passion for truth is asserted with the same vigor, but his personality is more complex; singular features have been moulded into absolute values, creating with powerful relief beings true to their essence. Characters constantly alike, haunting countenances of Christ or clowns, allusive landscapes, nebulous sceneries, as readily labelled slums in nightfall or Christ and his disciples; this ever-narrowing gamut is wide enough for him to convey the innumerable variations of the song of his soul.

His colours have undergone the same constriction. Whether a thickly laid impasto or light, unfettered hues, his coulours are always exalted, becoming — just as markedly as his shapes — an ever more active and significant emblem. They are the artist's specific mode of expression, penetrating deep into his being, wary that no tone be ever missed. Fierce, crude, exhaustive, his colouring is based on contrasts and oppositions and never on gradation of shades. Though faithful interpretations, they disregard all plastic effects, followed — by the apostrophe of his blacks and blues, the virulence of his reds and yellows, or by the ecstatic peacefulness of his green, orange and pink — the perplexing meanders of a passion hopelessly unrequited. Leaving nothing to chance, Rouault, as a master craftsman of old tradition and profound consciousness, stirs, kneads, churns the pigments, dosing his mixtures with infinite care until they become again traits, contours, tones, contrasts, "degradés" . . . each an original felicitous accomplishment.

The fact that so many scholars and prelates refuse to understand or to approach this art, proves most eloquently the echo and turmoil it rouses in the spirit of the beholder. His art — symbol and life — has created an absolute that has never been transcended. But above all, it has invested an epoch, regarded as amoral, with a sentimental and moral status, marking the gravity of a human verdict, the grandeur of man challenging his merciless destiny, which can no longer be ignored.

GASTON DIEHL, 1945

But beyond mere realism there was another reason for depicting the naked body stripped of the garments of antique harmony; and this, within the limits of language, I must examine, for it represents the last violent twist in the history of the nude.

Few more horrifying images have been put before us than paintings of naked prostitutes which Rouault executed in the years 1903—4. What has compelled the gentle pupil of G.M. to turn from biblical scenes and Rembrandtesque landscapes to these monsters of brutal depravity? Fundamentally, no doubt, the neo-Catholic doctrines of his friend Léon Bloy, by which on the lukewarm, materialistic society of 1900, absolute degradation came closer to redemption than wordly compromise. But the curious thing, for our present purpose, is that Rouault should have chosen to communicate this belief through the nude. He has done so precisely because it gives most pain. It has hurt him and he is savagely determined that it will hurt us. All those delicate feelings which flow together in our joy at the sight of an idealised human body, the Venus, shall we say, of Botticelli or of Giorgione, are shattered and profaned. The sublimation of desire is replaced by shame at its very existence; our dream, of a perfectible humanity is broken by this cruel reminder of what, in fact, man has contrived to make out of the raw material supplied to him in the cradle; and, from the point of view of form, all that was realised in the nude on its first creation, the sense of healthy structure, the clear, geometric shapes and their harmonious disposition, has been rejected in favour of lumps of matter, swollen and inert.

And yet Rouault convinces us that this hideous image is necessary. It is the ultimate antithesis of the Cnidian Venus, appearing rather late, after more than two thousand years, but none the less inevitable. All ideals are corruptible, and by 1903 the Greek ideal of physical beauty had suffered a century of singular corruption. A convincing assertion of complementary truth began, perhaps, in the drawing done by Degas in brothels; thus suggesting how the formal falsity of the academic nude was done, to some extent, a moral falsity for the amateurs who praised the nudes of Cabanel and Bouguereau had seen the real thing in the Maison Tellier. Degas' prostitutes are living beings, like obscene insects that convey the character of an epoch and a society. Rouault's figure belongs to a different world. Like the Cnidian Venus, she is an *objet de culte*, though of a religion closer to that of Mexico than of Cnidos. She is a monstrous idol inspiring us with fear rather than pity. In this respect Rouault is entirely unlike Rembrandt whom he so greatly admires, and who was his most fearless precursor in the exploitation of physical ugliness. Rembrand'ts approach was moral, Rouault's is religious. This is what gives his menacing prostitute her importance for us. Her hideous body is ideal because conceived in a spirit of awe.

KENNETH CLARK, 1957

Compact art, of unprecedented density, this volcanic lava possesses nothing alluring or agreeable (Matisse, at Chimiez, standing before two colour reproductions of Van Gogh and Rouault, hanging on a wall in his house, called my attention to the fact that *The Man with the Severed Ear*, compared to Rouault's *King David*, bore the air of a picture of the 18th century). Rouault's painting just like Daumier's art, misunderstood at his time, deliberately breaks with the canons of good taste.

Unlike Picasso (whose language glides without the slightest effort from geometrical abstraction to concrete figuration, asserting itself by its wealth of metamorphoses), Rouault's art tends to *present* (not represent) a condensed image of man. Though nourished with Mérovée and the old Byzantine masters whom he ably digested and transformed, Rouault, does not return to the subject, and yet for him man is still the central, dominating, haunting preoccupation. But, while man, the chief motif of representation, as a *noble subject* has always been and will, to my mind, be for ever, the external principle of Academic demonstration (it is for this reason that I abhor the word Humanism, which I fear we will never be able to reanimate without falling into the errors of Neo-Classicism), man for Rouault is a spiritual theme, the *raison d'être*, the object, not the subject, of the painting. Rouault's man is incorporated in the work, an integral part of each component element: ever present in love and brotherhood, in the glorification of the destitute and the labourer, in Christ mocked: *Ecce Homo*.

. . . .

The visual world was for Georges Rouault an immense moving surface whose shades, lights, colours, rhythms, either slow or fast, simple or complex were the result of an intense and incessant impulse stemming from the deepest recesses of the soul. His art implied no *problem of language*, since the language was an integral part of the act, like the art of a poet, who, utilizing common words, utters them with so profound a sense that the hackneyed vocable appears as a newly-forged word.

It is this, I feel, that distinguishes Rouault from the other painters of his generation, and in particular from Matisse who awarded so great an importance to conception. The mere fact that Rouault wished no one to speak about his craft or workmanship is easily comprehensible. What matters was not the means, but the end. For him, as for Claudel (Rouault confessed to me his sorrow that the poet of the *Cinq Grandes Odes* * showed no understanding for his work), art was but a means, its technique a pretext. Painting and poetry were for these two artists a language whose value lay not in itself, but rather in its power to impel the artist to express himself.

Rouault belonged to the spiritual family of Dante, Massaccio, Rembrandt; he was not a mirror reflecting nature as, for instance, Courbet had been, but rather a visionary possessing a transcendental image of reality, who invested everything he painted with a deep-piercing significance. This accounts for the lack of outward variety in his paintings, for the monotonous repetition of faces of clowns, "Veroniques", landscapes visited, whose worth resides in what they convey rather than what they picture.

In every one of his works, Rouault has set his seal. The paint is never inert. The artist never tired of kneading the substance with which he built up his painting, churning his pigments, casting and recasting every line and feature. It was indeed his hand, whose role he humbly accepted, that instilled into the painted matter the loftiest emotions. Never, however, did his hand guide his spirit. Supported by other artists for whom inner life prevailed over everything else, Georges Rouault was opposed to *homo faber* and to the artificial, fabricated beauty propounded by Valéry. He was not a virtuoso, nor a master according to the aesthetic tenets of the Renaissance. Just as with the artists of the Ravenna school, certain Roman sculptors, Giotto or Fra Angelico, it was faith that dominated and engendered everything. The outward beauty, physical harmony, this heritage from Greek-Roman paganism, had no impact upon this painter who readily sacrificed the beautiful, shapely proportions (and compositions symetrically balanced) to another dimension of a different essence, that is extant in a state of gestation in the restless and tormented matter in Van Gogh's canvases. A moral order is substituted

---

* Rouault was nevertheless sincerely moved, when, shortly before his death, Claudel proposed he should illustrate, his *Jeanne d'Arc*. The painter was at the time too weak to embark upon this task.

for a physical order, inner emotion for delectation, intense and significant life for spectacular pageantry.

PIERRE COURTHION, 1958

When Rouault turned his eyes away from the walls of galleries and museums and turned them upon life, the first things he met were clowns and prostitutes, which he set to portray in a manner completely different from his earlier mode. We refer in particular to his canvases *Prostitutes* (1903), *Head of Tragic Clown* (1904), *Prostitute* (1906), *Prostitute at Her Mirror* (1906) and *Odalisque* (1907). Though the change appeared as being sudden, it was in fact the fruit of a long gestation.

When Rouault mentioned his intention to go, like Cézanne, to the Midi, to paint "genuine motifs", Moreau dissuaded him. But after the death of his master, following Cézanne's example, he set to painting landscapes, learning thus to assess the relationship between the volume of images and the general effect of light and shade. What he particularly contrived to learn from Cézanne was the bold achievement of forms freed from all Academic canons, as well as the necessity of a coherent correlation of the elements of the picture, regardless of the external reality. His conception of space was likewise modified: his figures were no longer enclosed in a limited space; boundless and essentially the fruit of imagination, space was thenceforward subordinated to the characters. The artist thus created a free universe of phantasy and forms, similar to the one the Fauves were simultaneously evolving. It is for this reason that, though he did not belong to this group, his canvases were exhibited together with theirs.

. . . .

In order to understand the path followed by the painter in forging his new style, we must examine with particular attention his *Christ Mocked* in the Walter P. Chrysler Jr. Collection in New York, where the new tenets of his art clearly stand out. Alongside with the contour of the form, yet never coinciding, we perceive signs that symbolically represent the shadow of these contours. The image is less clear yet more vivid; its spiritual energy is all the more pregnant as it is less materially underscored. In many of his earlier *Heads of Christ*, the artist had preserved the traditional contours, diminishing thereby the intensity of the expression. The same principle governs also his colours, which are clear in this canvas, with its tonality in skyblue, rose, and extremely light yellows and greens. Though in that period Rouault worked principally in extremely sombre tones, he resorts in *Christ Mocked* to brighter colours in order to obtain, by contrast, a tragical effect. The relation between the spiritual emotion and the symbolic value of colours is no longer coincidental but contrasting. Lines and colours are ruled by a sort of ideographic style that might be named otherworldly or "of the other half". All material shapes, all tangible plastic elements have disappeared; the chromatic expression likewise has become indirect. Rouault achieves a formal expression of threatening terror by the destruction of form, just as he obtains the expression of torture by means of colours, which intrinsically signify joy. Beholding this canvas of *Christ Mocked*, one is apt to question the moral content of this picture. Pity is rendered too freely and intense to rouse compassion; it spells rather the uttermost revolt against the cruelty to which Christ was subjected. The almost joyful exaltation in his revolt strikes a lyrical note in the representation of cruelty, thereby stripping it of every element of brutality. The subject portrayed is Christ indeed, but the motif is reversed: it is the cruelty of man. That is why the "otherworldly" style corresponds so perfectly in its lines and colours with an emotional approach to Christ, because Christ likewise belongs to "the other world".

. . . .

Clowns are a theme particularly appropriate to illustrate the style of "the other world". It enables the artist to give full vent to his phantasy, inciting him to employ signs, lights and shades which, diminishing their brightness and precision, become more allusive and irrational. Two worthy examples of this manner are his *Illusionist*, dating from 1907 (Paris, Mme Simon Collection) and *Parade*, 1907 (Montreux, Baugerter Collection). The former is a masterpiece of luminist coherence and airiness, admirable by the detachment with which the artist treats his model, inaugurating an art almost independent of nature. The *Parade* stresses the grotesque element and evokes the pageantry more eloquently, despite the fanciful manner. It is indeed in the over-emphasis,

22

in the grotesque, that we realize the artist's denunciation of the vice and baseness of society, which are the relevant features of "the otherworldly style".

. . . . • . . . .

Rouault struggled with all his might to free himself from the fetters of Academism; he lived in spirit the religious revolution of Léon Bloy and unleashed all his wrath to brand the vices and hipocrisy of human society. Later realizing the necessity of striving beyond his caricatural hyperbole, he forged his hierographic "otherworldly" style, a style consistent with censorious assaults to which he however no longer resorted. Finally he succeeded in freeing himself from life's painful stranglehold reaching a state of perfect autonomy. He now evolved a style of constructive planes; between 1903 and 1918 he defined the essential "motifs" of his art and established the fundamental principles which henceforth he only needed to strengthen and develop.

. . . .

The ten years from 1930 to 1940 are rich in masterpieces. It should be remembered, as Rouault himself admitted, that he now worked out "motifs" that had been outlined before 1916. Their transformation however is so deep-going that we are constantly faced with new discoveries. The style which he had been forging up to 1930, compelled him to convert every line into a coloured area, enriching this colour with ever greater brilliance, so as to achieve not only a form but also a "motif" appropriate to the colour. Let's take as an example the famous picture of the *Old King* (Pittsburgh, Carnegie Institute). The first sketch goes back to 1916; the final version is one of the artist's most fabulous chromatic creations; but it took the artist twenty years to accomplish his initial vision. It is this phosphorescence, this impression of beholding a stained glass enclosed in a painting, which lends this image of the *Old King* not only its formal structure, but also its royal dignity, its grandeur and its melancholy. This phosphorescence, this novel quality of pigment, bursts forth all over the canvas. The superposition of successive layers of paint, the search for what Rouault called the "true tone", gave birth to something magical; indeed the light seems not to be content only to fall upon the canvas, it actually emerges from the canvas. Thus even when the tones are sombre they produce a luminous effect, by the brilliance of a light incorporated in the colours. It is this that renders Rouault's colours unique in the entire history of art. Rembrandt, Daumier, Cézanne, the great worshippers of light, which they have enriched with the deepest of shades, would be the first to recognize the virtue Rouault bequeathed to colour: the quality of phosphorescence.

. . . .

What rescued Rouault from Conformism was his rebellious spirit, the vital necessity to dedicate his entire religious faith not to the painting of seraphim but to proclaiming anathema against vice; seeking his Christian belief rather in the lives of clowns and destitutes than in religious rituals. His revolt must have been extremely profound to have been able to express in contemporary art an ideal and a faith worthy of the 13th century.

Such spiritual commandments inevitably called also for a rebellion in pictorial forms. Rouault waged battles on several planes: he first and foremost freed himself from the Academic tradition to avoid "schooled" art and to rediscover the prerequisites of Primitive Art, which does not however preclude "scholarly" art. He then developed the style which we have labelled "otherworldly", this modern style where the lines are independent of the contours, where shades prevail upon lights. Since 1903, there have been numerous discoveries of new forms, thanks principally to Cubism and Abstract Art. And, as though he had been living on another planet, Rouault's work displays not the slightest trace of the influence of his contemporaries. Certainly he, too, strove after a synthesis; by shedding the superfluous, adopting formal abbreviations and distortions that are a negation of realism, he finally evolved a transcendental form. It is by this personal and unique approach that he is radically different from the artists of his period. He may be labelled a French Expressionist; without, however, the slightest kinship with his German contemporaries, who, in their turn, felt the impulse and need of an Expressionist approach.

To join heaven and earth, the past and the present, realism and abstraction, image and the "otherworldly" style, intensity of tones with harmony of colour: this is the accomplishment of a moral conscience, clear-cut and trenchant like a diamond, an artist whose genius is growing unceasingly before our eyes.

LIONELLO VENTURI, 1959

Although it has never accurred to anyone to classify Rouault among the Impressionists, there have been many who consider him a typical Expressionist. But this painter cannot really be labelled. At the time of the Berlin exhibition in the Alfred Flechtheim Gallery, the German critics were prompt to point out his affinities with the *Brücke* group. Dr. Kurt Glaser observed that Rouault "rises well above his subject matter." The critic on the *Berliner Tageblatt* (was it Meier-Graefe?) asked rather shrewdly — the Expressionist movement was then at its height in Germany — if there had not been "a certain malice on the part of the organizers of the exhibition". Now he went on to say, "Everyone can see where all these emotional German artists found how to express themselves!" And the author of the article concluded — doubtless with Nolde, Kirchner, and even Jawlensky in mind (all three of whom were well-known in Germany at this time): It all comes from Rouault! The biting line, the ravaged faces, the compositions in which we always find two or three figures. Even the technique of dark brush strokes in black and touches of watercolor added here and there to lighten the whole."

PIERRE COURTHION, 1962

He descends from Goya, Daumier and somewhat from Degas, definitely from Toulouse-Lautrec: he belongs to the lineage of those attracted and obsessed by the stigmata of the human countenance and body.

Rouault first paints figures that we might call caricatural, degraded or aggresive, pitiful or awe-inspiring: clowns, prostitutes, judges, rickety children living in slums. On the one hand the judges, on the other the judged, the sentenced, the victims. His compassion, when he paints the latter is as evident and forceful as his scorn in depicting the others. Where does this wrath spring from? From his anguish, he admits it himself, the awe that seizes him at the thought that a human being is called to judge his fellow-man. The judge hence shall be judged too when his turn comes. So then he too can become the object of compassion. The gold and purple sun that casts fire into so many canvases — like pity warming man's heart — has not risen yet. A faint random ray of light flitters among the foul black toques, the soiled ermines, the scarlet robes as red as the victims' blood. Once these solemn ceremonial garments are removed, we uncover the body stripped of its pomp, no different from that of the prostitute under her gaudy finery, or the clown under his make up.

What prompts his appeal for clowns? The clown, too, is the wearer of a vestment, "a spangled costume"; suffice it for him to shed this costume for his soul to appear — in contrast with the glistening attire — steeped in "infinite sadness." Rouault cries out: "Strip all men of their glamorous spangled costumes." This is not what we might call a demystification, even if it be done for reasons of compassion. Rouault confesses: "I too am a clown"; indeed he painted a portrait of himself as a clown, but never in the guise of a judge. The clown and the mountebank's costume, is the response to a definite human need. It is the poor feast, the feast of the poor, to which flock all those who want to forget "the endless winters, the joyless days, as well as those with heartless and hostile visages, with sullen faces, and barren souls" — he declares in a sentence remindful of the cry of pathetic compassion uttered by Bernanos.

In becoming the iconographer of the **Holy Countenance**, Rouault's art takes on a new manner. His previous style, that might be called his lay period, comprising socially diversified figures, is marked at times by a freedom of lines, a sort of rambling drawing advancing in pursuit of itself, revolving around its own meanders, in curves, circles, and stripes, flying and dancing like a liana blown loose from its support. More than the body or face, Rouault is concerned with their motion. This rambling searching lasts until he moulds the image, around which the drawing shall settle. His unfinished works illustrate what Rouault could have attained; those who denounce his monotony, can now realize that in point of fact it is really a rejected diversity. In all the periods of his artistic life, what Rouault regarded as *unfinished*, is the moment when his line floats like a liana that has not yet found the tree to which it is willing to become its mere contour; the moment when shape and colour have not yet met their point of gravity (not immobility) and their fulfilment. *Finished*, means the moment the lines are cast, and flow into the mould of their final form, enveloping the countenance that carries the full message. The moment when the colours, no longer just the spangles of his circus shows, burst forth in transparent shadows of motion — intense, thick strokes of blue, red, yellow, green — like compact clods of furrowed earth or like the sun westering upon a sea turned golden by the fusion of a burning heart.

The airy windswept canvas is now replaced by an image bearing weight and indivisible matter, as heavy and unitary as a stained glass, a wooden icon, or the stone of an ex-voto. Far from being the starting-point, the centre of irradiation, the alluring reflex in a space of reflexes, the canvas becomes the focus, the point of convergence and condensation, the concentration of a storage. Motion and gaze have found their rest, their orbit. What we are offered is not an idol, not even a Byzantine Christ. It is a revived Roman image of Christ. Rouault succeeded in limning Christ as a Holy Countenance, at once isolated from the world, immutable, and yet a human image conscious of all that is human, responding to our solitude, our suffering, our aspirations. This hieratic woodenlike icon, narrates our story, foreshadowing our passion. This thick impasto, these weighty pigments evoke the earth just as our flesh is earth. What weighs as heavy as lead, what burns like the oil in the lamp, these bluish waves on the water, these velvet stretches of sky, this stifling noontide over the Dead Sea in the scorching, breezeless heat, is nought but the weight of the soul in the flames of its Orient, and the oil trickles off the painter's brush, drop by drop, just like gems borne out of their fire, resin turned into glazing pearls.

GAËTAN PICON, 1969

If Matisse bestows full autonomy to colour, if Pablo Picasso forges a new perspective, Rouault in the early years of the 20th century, breaks asunder the contours, unleashing a shower of blazing tones. His violence exceeds that of Mathias Grünewald, Goya, Van Gogh, Edvard Munch, Ensor and of Kokoschka, Soutine and Nolde. Though he does not deny the capital conquests of contemporary art, Rouault breaks away from the Fauves and the Cubists, to whom he owes nothing. He pursues a road of his own. An artist unfettered by conventions, he fears not to tackle the boldest of ventures.

Since Delacroix, Rouault is the sole painter whose intellectual bent and spiritual affinities are worthy of note. Yet, where — as the master of the *Crusaders*, derived his inspiration from mythology, ancient or modern history, from the theatre and poetry, Rouault, though not a painter of literary inspiration, created characters. His personages are eternal types, like those of Rabelais, Mathurin Régnier, Scarron, Molière, Lesage, Fernand Crommelynick and Jarry . . .

Numerous historians claim that the septuagenarian has lost his erstwhile frenzy and that his holy wrath no longer inspires his work. Is it the discovery of his inner life that has chased away his gloom? Has he found the path of reconciliation with life . . . This novel serenity, or at least, this moment of relaxation are, truly speaking, empty words. The picture we are witnessing is that of the fulfilment of a personality about to attain its acme. Like Cézanne, Renoir and Bonnard, similar too to the great princes of ancient painting — Titian and Rembrandt — Georges Rouault achieved the transmutation of his raw material. This thaumaturgist blends painting with prayer and prayer with poetry. His manner has grown heavier, made up of agglutinated clots. The artist's palette is dominated by chrome yellow alongside carmine and Veronese green. Fantastic flowers make their appearance.

Rouault's pigments are clay burnt in a furnace. This colour does not adhere to a shape, but creates a shape indirectly, gaining such relief that it becomes perceptible to the touch. The graphic structure has disappeared. In its stead there is a magma of pigments. The "motif" emerges from this fusion of agglutinated tones, brutally applied or spread with the palette-knife on the canvas.

It was only Rembrandt in his later works who went so far along the path of an art stripped of all illusion adopting a manner that can be labelled Tachism or an informal style. And yet neither Rembrandt, nor Rouault is a dreamer raking the ashes. This magician, or alchemist, is an artisan who kneads his coloured substance with the secret thought of producing a world of images and countenances that should force man to contemplation.

WALDEMAR GEORGE, 1971

CHRONOLOGY
AND CONCORDANCES

1871 May 27, Georges Rouault was born in Paris, 51 Rue de la Villette, Belleville, in a
cellar, on the last day of the Commune, while the battle was still raging in the city.
His father, a native of Brittany, was a cabinet-maker by trade, employed, at the time,
at the Pleyel piano factory. His mother, a Parisian, was the daughter of a post office
clerk, Alexandre Champdavoine — a self-educated man, keen on Literature and the
Arts, a reader of Goethe and Spinoza, and ardent admirer of Rembrandt, Courbet,
Daumier and Manet.
Birth of Theodor Pallady

1872—1885 Spends the early years of his childhood mostly in the home of his grandfather
Champdavoine; the latter, realizing that his grandson is keen on drawing, takes young
Rouault to museums and to the book-sellers on the Quais of the Seine where he buys
reproductions of the works of his favourite painters.
Attends the primary classes, first, in a Protestant Institution and then, in the Communal
School obtaining his certificate for elementary studies.

1874 *Paris. First exhibition of the Impressionists.*

1879 *Death of Daumier.*

1880 *Birth of Franz Marc and E. L. Kirchner.*

1881 *Birth of Picasso.*

1882 *Birth of Georges Braque.*

1885—1890 Alexandre Champdavoine dies in an accident. Forced to earn his living, Rouault
serves an apprenticeship with Tamoni, a stained glass painter, and then is engaged by
Hirsch to work on the restoration of medieval windows. He attends at the same time
the evening classes of the École des Arts Décoratifs, founded in 1887. Here his drawings
are remarked by the painter Albert Besnard who commissions him to execute the
stained glass windows for the École de Pharmacie after his cartoons. Rouault refuses
the offer out of loyalty to his master Hirsch.

1886 *Last exhibition of the Impressionists.*

1887 *Birth of August Macke.*

1890 December 3. Determined to follow his calling, enters the École des Beaux-Arts, in the
studio of Elie Delaunay, while still working on stained glass with Hirsch.
Death of Van Gogh.

1891 Paints a series of religious subjects, treated in a Rembrandtesque style.
*September 5. Elie Delaunay dies: Gustave Moreau is appointed in his place. The latter, an
excellent educationalist stimulates the development of the personality of his students, among whom
Matisse, Marquet, Theodor Pallady.* Rouault becomes his favourite student.

1892 March 13. Passes the final tests to be admitted as regular student in the Painting
Department of the École des Beaux-Arts. Is awarded a school prize for his studio works.
Leaves Hirsch in order to devote himself exclusively to painting.

1893 March 31. On Moreau's advice competes for the "Prix de Rome", with his composition
The Ordeal of Samson. He fails. The prize is awarded to one of Gérôme's pupils.
The Vollard Gallery is inaugurated.

1894 February 6. Competes for the Fortin d'Ivry prize and wins the Second Medal for his
composition *Coriolanus in the House of Tullius.*
June. First prize at the Chenavard competition for his work *The Child Jesus Among the
Doctors.*

1895 Competes for the "Prix de Rome", for the second time, with his composition *The Dead
Christ Mourned by the Holy Women,* but the prize goes to one of Bonnat's pupils.
Following this failure, Moreau advises him to leave the school and work alone. Under
the name of Rouault Champdavoine, makes his début at the Salon des Artistes Français
with his painting *The Child Jesus Among the Doctors.* The critics are generally favourable.

1896 Exhibits at the Salon des Artistes Français.
Performance of Jarry's "Ubu Roi" at the Théâtre de l'Oeuvre.

1897 Exhibits at the Salon "Rose Croix" (*Rosa Croce*) and at the Salon des Artistes Français.
Paints romantic landscapes, with sacred or lay scenes which mark a break with his
previous subjects.

1898 April 18. *Gustave Moreau dies: he bequeathes his studio and collection to the Government, on
condition they be transformed into a museum bearing his name.*
Rouault is deeply affected by the death of his mentor; a period of moral and material
adversities.

1899 Exhibits at the Salon des Artistes Français.

1900 Exhibitions at the Salon des Artistes Français. Obtains a Bronze Medal at the Paris World Fair.

1901 April. Retires to Ligugé, where Huysmans plans to set up, at the Benedictine Monastery, a brotherhood of artists whose activity should be carried out in an atmosphere of lofty spirituality, removed from worldly temptations, publicity and honours; but the Law prohibiting the foundation of Societies enacted in July, puts an end to these plans. Rouault returns to Paris, strengthened in his resolution to make no concession to the public taste. Exhibits at the Salon des Artistes Français.
Death of Toulouse-Lautrec.

1902 For reasons of ill health, spends a time in the Haute Savoie. This period of solitude as well as the reading of Léon Bloy's two novels *La Femme Pauvre* and *Le Mendiant Ingrat*, found in Moreau's library, aid him to renew his vision. Pivoting round social themes, he paints mostly circus scenes, figures of clowns, acrobats, prostitutes, by which he denounces with rabid vehemence the injustices prevalent in the world he lives in. His works are principally gouaches and watercolours in predominantly blue tones.
Exhibits for the first time at the Salon des Indépendants in which he henceforth participates regularly up to 1912.

1903 January 14. The inauguration of the Georges Moreau Museum; Georges Rouault is appointed curator. Together with Matisse, Marquet, Bonnard and others founds the Salon d'Automne, displaying two canvases at the inaugural exhibition; participates in the exhibitions of this Salon up to 1908.
Franz Marc visits Paris and Brittany.
Death of Gauguin and Pissarro.

1904 Meets Léon Bloy, to whom he becomes deeply attached, despite the difference of views in matters of art. The 8 oil paintings and 36 pastels and watercolours (crepuscular landscapes, clowns, wrestlers, etc) on show at the Salon d'Automne, provoke — by their sombre cast the hilarity and indignation of both public and critics.

1905 At the Salon d'Automne exhibits his triptych *Prostitutes*. One of the panels, entitled *Monsieur and Madame Poulot*, characters inspired from Léon Bloy's *La Femme Pauvre*, causes the indignation of the writer. Three of his paintings are exhibited in the hall reserved to the Fauves.
E. L. Kirchner, E. Heckel, K. Schmidt-Routtluff, set up "Die Brücke" group in Dresden.

1906 Exhibits at the Berthe Weill Gallery. Makes the acquaintance of the ceramist André Méthey, for whom he was subsequently to work until 1912.
Death of Cézanne.

1907 At Méthey's, meets Vollard who purchases some of Rouault's ceramic pieces; the latter commissions Rouault to work exclusively for him.
Accompanied by a friend, the State Attorney Granier, visits the lawcourts where he makes sketches and drawings of judges; his types become the very emblems of an unjust society. This theme is intensely exploited until 1914.
Picasso paints "Les Demoiselles d'Avignon".
Macke visits Paris. Death of J. K. Huysmans.

1908 January 27. Marries the sister of the painter Georges Le Sidaner, the pianist Marthe Le Sidaner by whom he was to have four children: Geneviève, Isabelle, Michel and Agnès.
The first Abstract paintings by Kandinsky.

1910 One-man show at the Druet Gallery (121 paintings, 8 drawings and 53 ceramic pieces).

1911 Moves to Versailles. Close friendship with Jacques and Raïssa Maritain, and with André Suarès. Tackles the theme of the Exodus which he reproduces in several variants.
December. Exhibition at the Druet Gallery.
Exhibition of the Cubist painters at the Salon des Indépendants.

1912 Third one-man show at the Druet Gallery.

1913 Ambroise Vollard buys Rouault's entire production.

1914 April 14. Moves to Paris again. The themes of prostitutes and judges become less prominent in his work.

1914—1916 Devotes most of his time to etching. Begins the illustration of Vollard's book *Les Réincarnations du Père Ubu* on which he was to work for 14 years, producing 22 aquatints and 144 woodcuts.
Embarks upon the series of etchings *Miserere et Guerre* in which he treats the "theme of death and resurrection"; initially planned to appear in two volumes, comprising fifty plates each, the etchings are published only in 1948 in a single volume. At about the same time he begins two cycles of woodcuts, *Paysages légendaires* and *Petite Banlieu*, as well as a series of individual etchings.

1916 *The Beginning of Ozenfant and Le Corbusier's Purist Movement.*
Death of Franz Marc. First manifestation of the Dada group at Zürich.

1917 Signs an agreement with Vollard, whereby all his present and future production is ceded to the picture-dealer. In order to be able to complete the hundreds of unfinished works, which he constantly keeps retouching, Ambroise Vollard sets up a studio for him on the top floor of his house, paying him an annuity, ensuring his subsistance.
Death of Léon Bloy and Degas.

1918 His subjects change from social to religious themes dominated by Christ's countenance. His palette becomes more luminous.
Death of Apollinaire.

1919 His canvas *The Child Jesus Among the Doctors* is acquired by the government and placed in the Colmar Museum — this is Rouault's first painting to be purchased for a public collection.

1920 One-man show at "La Licorne" Gallery.
First Dada exhibition in Paris.

1921 Michel Puy publishes the first monograph dedicated to Rouault in the collection "Les Peintres Français Nouveaux".

1922 One-man show at the Barbazanges Gallery.

1924 Retrospective exhibition at the Druet Gallery (88 paintings and 8 enamels). The artist is awarded the Légion d'Honneur.

1925 Exhibits at Berlin and Düsseldorf.

1926 One-man show at the "Galerie des Quatre Chemins".
Brings out the volume *Souvenirs intimes* illustrated with a series of lithographs and with a preface by André Suarès.

1927 One-man show at the Bing Gallery.

1929 Exhibition of watercolours and gouaches at the "Galerie des Quatre Chemins".
Designs the settings and costumes for Diaghileff's ballet *The Prodigal Son,* with score by Prokofiev. During a short stay in Switzerland suffers an accident causing severe burns on his hands.

1930 No longer writes the date of his works. His subjects are predominantly religious scenes, evoking characters from the Old Testament; likewise circus scenes: families of clowns, mountebanks and equestriennes.
Exhibitions in London (St. George's Gallery), München (Neumann Gallery), New York (Drummer Gallery), Chicago (Art Club).

1931 Exhibits in New York (Demotte Gallery), Brussels (Schwartzenberg Gallery), Geneva (Musée de l'Athénée).
"Abstraction-Creation" Group is founded by Mondrian and Pevsner in Paris.

1932 Executes tapestry cartoons for the Aubusson Factory *(Wounded Clown, The Little Family).*
His vision grows brighter. Paints flowers and sun-flooded landscapes.

1933 Exhibition in New York.

1935 Exhibition in London and Northampton.

1936 Exhibits at "Le Portique" Gallery.

1937 June-October. Sends 42 canvases to the Exhibition "Les Maîtres de l'Art Contemporain", held at the Petit Palais during the World Fair. This retrospective exhibition, including works from 1905, is a revelation for both public and critics, determining Lionello Venturi to devote an important study to Rouault, published in New York, in 1940.
One-man show in New York.
The Church Notre-Dame-de-Toutes Grâces is being built at Assy (Savoie) after Novarina's plans.

1938 Exhibition of etchings in New York (Museum of Modern Art) and at Basel (Kunsthalle), together with Vlaminck and Dufy.
Paris: International Exhibition of the Surrealists.

1939 July 22. Ambroise Vollard dies following a car accident; Rouault is deeply affected but also anxious for the fate of his unfinished works, left in the workshop of the art-dealer's house.
August. The Second World War breaks out. Rouault retires with his family to Beaumont-sur-Sarthe where he owns a small property. Exhibits at New York (Bignon Gallery and Pierre Matisse Gallery).

1940—1941 Moves to Golfe Juan to escape from the dangers of the war. Exhibitions at Los Angeles (Datzell-Hatfield Gallery), Boston (Institute of Modern Art), Washington (Philipp Memorial Gallery), San Francisco (Museum of Art), New York (Marie Harriman Gallery).

1942 Returns to Paris. Tries without avail to recuperate his unfinished works; failing to obtain them brings an action against Ambroise Vollard's heirs.
April. One-man show at Louis Carré Gallery, displaying the works painted at Golfe Juan.

1943 Brings out the volume *Divertissement* containing principally circus scenes.

1945 Wide-ranging retrospective exhibition in New York (Museum of Modern Art). He is commissioned 5 stained glass windows for the Church in Assy, for the decoration of which Matisse, Lurçat, Léger, Bazaine and Germaine Richier are likewise called upon. The windows are completed in 1947.

1946 Exhibition in London (The Tate Gallery) and in Paris (Bing and Druin galleries) together with Braque.

1947 March 19. Wins the case against Vollard's heirs who are ordered to return some 800 works left in the workshop. 119 of these had already been sold by the art-dealer's heirs.
Exhibits at Prague (Club of Intellectuals Gallery) a set of 10 paintings and 25 etchings; likewise in Paris (Galerie Odette des Garets) and in New York. Brings out the album *Stella Vespertina* containing 100 works on religious subjects.
Death of Bonnard and Marquet.

1948 April. Wide-ranging retrospective exhibition with 266 works at Zürich (Kunsthaus).
The French Government exhibits 26 paintings and 12 etchings by Rouault at the Venice Biennial.
November 5. As an evidence of his moral integrity, in the presence of a representative of the Ministry of Justice and of the film cameras, Rouault destroys 315 works which he regarded as inadequate, from the collection of unfinished works, returned to him by virtue of the Court Writ.
Presentation of the entire cycle *Miserere* at the Odette des Garets Gallery.
Death of André Suarès. Exhibition of Abstract Art at the Galerie des Deux Iles.
1949 September. First models for the enamels to be executed at Ligugé, in the Abbey workshop.
1949—1950 An itinerant exhibition, comprising 26 paintings and drawings is held in several cities in France and abroad: Buenos Aires (Witcomb Gallery), Rome, Florence, Milan, as part of the Exhibition of French Sacred Art.
1950 One-man show in Paris (Masigny Gallery) with early works.
Dewasne and Pillet found the "Académie de l'Art Abstrait" in Paris.
1951 June 6. Celebrating the artist's eightieth birthday, the Centre Catholique des Intellectuals Français organizes a "Tribute to Rouault" at the Palais Chaillot, including the first public showing of the film "Miserere". Exhibits in Paris (Galerie de France) 10 enamels made at Ligugé; the same are displayed in Stockholm (Samlaren Galery) and in Göteborg (Art Museum).
The second presentation of the *Miserere* cycle at the Louis Carré Gallery.
1952 Retrospective Exhibition in Brussels (Palais des Beaux-Arts), Amsterdam (Musée Municipal) and Paris (Musée National d'Art Moderne) containing most of the exhibits displayed at Zürich in 1948.
1953 Retrospective Exhibition in the United States: Cleveland (Museum of Art), New York (Museum of Modern Art), Los Angeles (County Museum) and in Japan at Tokyo and Osaka.
Death of Dufy, Picabia and Albert Gleizes.
1954 Retrospective Exhibition in Milan (Modern Art Gallery).
Death of Henri Matisse and Fernand Léger.
1955 One-man show at Jerusalem (Jezabel National Museum).
1956 One-man show at Albi (Toulouse-Lautrec Museum) and Paris (Creuzevault Gallery).
1957 One-man show of enamels at Rome (Odyssia Gallery).
1958 February 13. Georges Rouault dies. Memorial Exhibition at Fribourg (Musée d'Art et d'Histoire), Lausanne (Galerie Vallotton), Paris (Bibliothèque Nationale and Galerie Le Garrec), Tokyo (Mitzue). Rouault's works are likewise on show at the exhibition of "Modern Sacred Art" held at the Municipal Museum in Delft.

BIBLIOGRAPHY

APOLLINAIRE, GUILLAUME: *Chronique d'art* (1902—1910), Gallimard, Paris, 1960
BLUNT, ANTHONY: *Rouault*, in *The Spectator*, 1935, October 18
CLARK, KENNETH: *The Nude. A Study of Ideal Art*, John Murray, London, 1957
COURTHION, PIERRE: *Georges Rouault*, including a catalogue made up in collaboration with Isabelle Rouault, Flammarion, Paris, 1962
DIEHL, GASTON: *Georges Rouault*, in *Les Problèmes de la Peinture*, Confluences, Paris, 1945
DORIVAL, BERNARD: *Préface*, in G e o r g e s   R o u a u l t: *Sur l'art et sur la vie*, Denoël-Gonthier, Paris, 1971
EINSTEIN, KARL: *Georges Rouault*, Berlin 1931
GEORGE, WALDEMAR: *Génie et destin de Rouault*, Paris 1971.
KAHN, GUSTAVE: in *Mercure de France*, 1912, January 16, Ap. L i o n e l l o   V e n t u r i, *Rouault*, Skira Geneva, 1959
LHOTE, ANDRÉ: *La peinture. Le cœur et l'esprit*, Denoël et Steele, Paris, 1933
MALRAUX, ANDRÉ: *Notes sur l'expression tragique en peinture à propos des œuvres récentes de Rouault*, in *Formes*, 1930 December 1
MARITAIN, JACQUES: *Chronique de la Quinzaine. Georges Rouault*, in *La Revue Universelle*, 1924, May 15
MARX, ROGER: *Salon des Champs Elysées*, in *La Revue Encyclopédique*, 1896, Ap. L i o n e l l o   V e n t u r i: *Rouault*, Skira, Geneva, 1959
PACH, WALTER: *Georges Rouault*, in *Parnassus*, 1933 January
PICON, GAËTAN: *Les Lignes de la Main*, Nouvelle Revue Française, Paris, 1969
ROUAULT, GEORGES: *Sur l'Art et sur la Vie*, Denoël Gonthier, Paris 1971
ROUAULT, GEORGES — SUARÈS, ANDRÉ: *Correspondance*, Gallimard, Paris, 1960
SWEENEY, JAMES J.: *Rouault's still remains no easy beauty*, in *New York Times*, 1930, April 6
VAUXCELLES, LOUIS: *Salon d'Automne*, in *Gil Blas*, 1904, October 14, Ap. L i o n e l l o   V e n t u r i, *Rouault*, Skira, Geneva, 1959
VENTURI, LIONELLO: *Rouault*, Skira, Geneva, 1959
ZAHAR, MARCEL: *Georges Rouault ou le Retour au Grotesque Dramatique*, in *Formes*, No. 31, 1933

LIST OF ILLUSTRATIONS

In the text:

STUDY
Pen drawing
1885
École Nationale des Arts Décoratifs
Paris

MISERERE ★
(Variant of Plate No. 18)
"The Condemned is Gone..."
Wash-tint
55×38 cm.

DRAWING FOR "UBU"
China ink
1918
Private Collection, Paris

PLATE FOR
"LES RÉINCARNATIONS DU
PÈRE UBU"
by Ambroise Vollard
1928

Plates

1. THE RETURN
   OF THE PRODIGAL SON
   Charcoal drawing
   1852
2. THE ORDEAL OF SAMSON
   Oil
   146×114 cm.
   1893
   County Museum, Los Angeles
3. CORIOLANUS IN THE HOUSE
   OF TULLIUS
   (Competition of Pained Sketches)
   February 1894
   Oil
   46×38 cm.
   École Nationale des Beaux-Arts, Paris
4. THE DEAD CHRIST MOURNED BY
   THE HOLY WOMEN
   (Competition for the Prix de Rome)
   Oil
   114×146 cm.
   1895
   Art Museum, Grenoble
5. BATHERS
   Watercolour
   44×33 cm.
   1903
   Private Collection, Paris
6. DANCING THE CHAHUT
   (À TABARIN)
   Watercolour and pastel

70×54 cm.
1905
Musée d'Art Moderne de la Ville de
Paris
7. PROSTITUTE AT HER MIRROR
   Watercolour
   72×55 cm.
   1906
   Musée National d'Art Moderne, Paris
8. STREET FAIR WRESTLERS
   Watercolour and pencil
   1906
   Private Collection, U.S.A.
9. THE SKATING RINK ★
   Ink and oil on paper
   55×66 cm.
   c. 1900—1906
   Musée National d'Art Moderne, Paris
10. DRUNKEN WOMAN
    Watercolour and pastel
    70×54 cm.
    1905
    Musée d'Art Moderne de la Ville de
    Paris
11. NUDE
    Sketch
    Oil
    61×44 cm.
    1905
    Philippe Leclercq Collection,
    Hem, France
12. CHRIST MOCKED
    Oil
    114×78.5 cm.
    1905
    Walter P. Chrysler Jr. Collection,
    New York
13. THE CONJUROR
    Oil and watercolour
    44×33 cm.
    1907
    Mme Henri Simon Collection, Paris
14. HEAD OF CLOWN
    Oil
    39×31 cm.
    c. 1907
    Private Collection, U.S.A.
15. MONSIEUR ET MADAME POULOT
    Watercolour and gouache
    70×52 cm.
    1905
    Philippe Leclercq Collection,
    Hem, France
16. PARADE
    Watercolour and pastel
    65×105 cm.
    1907
    Kunstmuseum, Basel

★ Unfinished work donated to the French Government

17. PROSTITUTES
Watercolour and pastel
70×50 cm.
1906
18. ODALISQUE
Watercolour
64×98 cm.
1907
Bangerter Collection, Montreux
19. THE COURT
Watercolour and gouache
30×20 cm.
1908
Private Collection, Winterthur
20. PARC DE VERSAILLES,
THE STAIRCASE (THE TERRACE)
Watercolour
67×52 cm.
1910
Musée National d'Art Moderne, Paris
21. SILHOUETTE
OF A WOMAN WITH A SMALL DOG
Ink, watercolour and pastel
27×21 cm.
1908
Private Collection, Paris
22. CARRIED AWAY
Watercolour
19×31 cm.
1908
Private Collection, Paris
23. LANDSCAPE (THE BARGE)
Oil
36×50 cm.
c. 1910—1912
Private Collection, Paris
24. VILLAGE IN THE SNOW
Crayon and volatile oil
16×31 cm.
c. 1912
Private Collection, Winterthur
25. WINTER LANDSCAPE
Gouache
16×31 cm.
c. 1912
Hanloser Collection, Winterthur
26. THE WRESTLER
Ink and watercolour
39.5×30.5 cm.
c. 1913
Musée d'Art Moderne de la Ville de Paris
27. TICKET SELLER *
Watercolour and gouache on paper
39×30.5 cm.
c. 1907—1910
Musée National d'Art Moderne, Paris
28. MONSIEUR LOYAL WITH RED VEST *
Oil on paper mounted on canvas
31×20 cm.
Musée National d'Art Moderne, Paris
29. MEN OF JUSTICE
Watercolour and coloured ink
30×19
c. 1913
Musée d'Art Moderne de la Ville de Paris
30. THE HOVEL
Gouache, tempera and pencil
31×19 cm.
c. 1913

Musée d'Art Moderne de la Ville de Paris
31. NUDE
Wash-tint
c. 1917
Private Collection
32. NUDE
Wash
38.5×23.5 cm.
1917
Private Collection, Winterthur
33. SELF-PORTRAIT
Volatile oil
1921
Georges Rouault studio
34. EQUESTRIENNE
Gouache
47×39 cm.
Private Collection, Paris
35. VERSAILLES (THE TERRACE)
Oil and gouache
Georges Rouault Studio
36. LADY OF FASHION *
Ink, gouache and pastel
on paper mounted on canvas
c. 1929
Musée National d'Art Moderne, Paris
37. PARADE *
Wash-tint on paper mounted on canvas
74×103 cm.
Musée National d'Art Moderne, Paris
38. THE REAPERS *
Wash-tint and coloured ink
29.5×46 cm.
Musée National d'Art Moderne, Paris
39. MISERERE
(Plate No. 16)
"Lady of High Society Thinks She Can
Take a Reserved Seat for Heaven"
Copper-plate etching
50×35 cm.
1922
40. MISERERE
(Plate No. 8)
"Don't We All Wear Make-up?"
Copper-plate etching
66×42.5 cm.
1927
41. EXODUS
Wash-tint
Georges Rouault Studio
42. PROSTITUTE AND SOLDIERS
(Sketch for *Miserere*) *
Wash-tint on tracing-paper mounted on canvas
60.5×45.5 cm.
Musée National d'Art Moderne, Paris
43. THE WORKMAN'S APPRENTICE
(SELF-PORTRAIT)
Oil
66×52 cm.
1925
Musée National d'Art Moderne, Paris
44. DECORATIVE FLOWERS
Oil
62×53.5 cm.
1946
Musée National d'Art Moderne, Paris

45. THE MILLER *
Wash, China ink and coloured inks
66×49 cm
Musée National d'Art Moderne, Paris

46. REMEMBRANCE FROM
FLANDERS *
China ink and pastel
on paper mounted on canvas
100×74.5 cm.
c. 1928—1930
Musée National d'Art Moderne, Paris

47. SOLITUDE
Oil
79×54 cm.
c. 1937
Former Ambroise Vollard Collection,
Paris

48. STUDY OF HEAD *
Volatile oil on paper mounted on canvas
31×19 cm.
Musée National d'Art Moderne, Paris

49. DANCE STEP *
Volatile oil, watercolour and pastel
on paper mounted on canvas
45×33 cm.
Musée National d'Art Moderne, Paris

50. FLIGHT INTO EGYPT,
TREES AND HILLS
Gouache and coloured inks
on paper mounted on canvas
47×75 cm.
Musée National d'Art Moderne, Paris

51. MISERERE
(Sketch for unfinished plate)
Oil on engraving
57×44 cm.
Musée National d'Art Moderne, Paris

52. THE OLD KING
Oil
77×54 cm.
1937
Carnegie Institute, Pittsburgh

53. JUDGE
1937

54. INTERIOR OF A CHURCH
IN BRITTANY
Oil
70.5×108 cm.
1938

55. "RUSSALKA"
Gouache
1941
Tériade Collection, France

56. DANCERS
Gouache
28×22.5 cm.
1941
Tériade Collection, France

57. JOAN OF ARC
Oil
67×48 cm.
1948—1949
Private Collection, Paris

58. THE HOLY COUNTENANCE
Oil
91×65 cm.
1933
Musée National d'Art Moderne, Paris

59. THE LITTLE FAMILY
Oil
208×116 cm.
1932
Private Collection, Paris

60. EXODUS *
Wash and China ink on paper mounted
on canvas
30×42 cm.
Musée National d'Art Moderne, Paris

61. AUTUMN
Oil
68×105 cm.
1948
Vatican Museum, Rome

62. ITALIAN WOMAN
The Tate Gallery, London

63. THE THREE JUDGES
Oil
78×64 cm.
1936
Tate Gallery, London

64. MARGOT
Gouache
30.5×24 cm.
1941
Tériade Collection, France

65. HEAD OF CLOWN
Oil
66×48 cm.
1948
Museum of Fine Arts, Boston

66. LITTLE PAGEBOY
IN RED AND GOLD
Gouache
31×25 cm.
1941
Tériade Collection, France

67. SKETCH FOR
"LES FLEURS DU MAL"
(FRONTISPIECE)
China ink and gouache
Georges Rouault Studio

68. DECORATIVE FLOWERS
Gouache
Georges Rouault Studio

69. PIERROT
Thomson Collection, Pittsburgh

70. GILLES
Oil
66×47 cm.
c. 1939
Philippe Leclercq Collection,
Hem, France

71. "MAN IS WOLF TO MAN"
Oil
56×46 cm.
c. 1948
Musée National d'Art Moderne
Paris

72. TWILIGHT
Oil
76.5×56 cm.
c. 1937—1938
Beyler Collection, Basel

73. CHRISTIAN NOCTURNE
Oil on canvas
97×52 cm.
1972
Musée National d'Art Moderne, Paris

1. The Return of the Prodigal Son

2. The Ordeal of Samson
3. Coriolanus in the House of Tullius

8. Street Fair Wrestlers

9. The Skating Rink

16. Parade

23. Landscape

24. Village in the Snow
25. Winter Landscape

28. Monsieur Loyal with Red Vest

31. Nude
32. Nude

34. Equestrienne
35. Versailles (The Terrace)

39. Miserere (Plate No. 16)
   "Lady of High Society Thinks She Can Take a Reserved Seat for Heaven"
40. Miserere (Plate No. 8) "Don't We All Wear Make-up?"
←

41. Exodus

42. Prostitute and Soldiers

45. The Miller
46. Remembrance from Flanders

53. Judge

55. "Russalka"

56. Dancers

57. Joan of Arc
58. The Holy Countenance

59. The Little Family

64. Margot

65. Head of Clown

66. Little Pageboy in Red and Gold

67. Sketch for "Les Fleurs du Mal" (Frontispiece)

68. Decorative Flowers
69. Pierrot

70. Gilles
71. "Man is Wolf to Man"

72. Twilight
73. Christian Nocturne

MERIDIANE PUBLISHING HOUSE
BUCHAREST

PRINTED IN ROMANIA